Teach your children to read well and easy

by Ana Leblanc

ALL COPYRIGHTS RESERVED 2017

The information herein is offered for informational purposes solely, and is universal as so. The presentation of the information is without contract or any type of guarantee assurance.

PREFACE

It is truly amazing how fast children can learn different things. Their minds are constantly turning, trying to figure things out. They are trying to take in as much information as they possibly can. Unfortunately, not all of this knowledge is what we as parents think is acceptable material.

There is so much negative material in the world these days. Parents have to watch almost everything that their children are into. None of us want are children to learn from the wrong influence. It is important for us to be the main teachers in their lives. Due to this, we have to find more creative and interesting ways for children learning.

One of the main aspects to learning is reading. It is an amazing and sometimes complicated adventure. In order to keep children interested, we need to keep things simple and fun. You can always tell when they become bored with something because it turns into a big fight to get them to do what we need and want them to do. For this reason, we need to make sure that learning to read never becomes tedious and boring.

Children love the opportunity to be the center of attention, so why not allow them to be through reading. We can show them how special they are, while actually teaching them to read. Not a lot of children like to learn if they know it is learning. So, disguise it to make it fun and they will learn faster than ever.

As a parent, there is no doubt that you want the very best for your children. That is probably the main reason why you want to teach your son and daughter how to read at a very young age. You hopes that by doing so, you will be giving them a competitive advantage when it is time for them to go to school.

If you are trying to help your child develop his or her reading skills,then this is a must read book. In this book, I am going to share with you a few tips and strategies that can make a big difference to the progress of your child

Table of Contents

CHAPTER 1- CHILDREN AND LEARNING

How would you like a way to help your child to feel more successful at home, at school, with friends?

How would you like to feel less stress in your life and have a better relationship with your child?

What if your child knew simple, effective strategies that will enable him to learn easily and quickly?

It has been my experience that virtually every young person that I have worked with has had the desire to do well, to be accepted by their peers, to feel pride from their parents, and to feel good about themselves. If they are not doing well in school or with learning, it is not because they lack the desire to learn. The number one problem that I find children and adolescents facing is that they don't have effective strategies for learning the information that is being taught to them.

When children feel that they don't learn well, it often affects their self-esteem significantly. As a result, many young people will not only experience problems around learning, but also self-esteem issues, emotional and behavioral problems, social skills problems, anxiety, depression, or family issues. Virtually every aspect of their life is affected.

Our public schools, unfortunately, often work from the assumption that a student already knows how to learn and therefore focus on teaching content rather than on the process of learning. Most students learn as they go along, figure out what works, and modify their strategies as they go. Many, though, have never learned effective strategies for learning; they often use strategies that take a long time and simply do not work, and they struggle in school. Students need strategies for how to learn, not just what to learn so they don't have to continue to struggle.

The most effective learning strategy for academics is a visual learning strategy. Tasks such as learning spelling words, math facts, memorizing facts and data and learning vocabulary words are learned more easily and quickly if the student learns them visually. When students learn visually, they tend to be more interested and learn □uickly and easily. When they don't learn visually, they tend to struggle. The very first thing to address is the student's perception of his ability to learn and use his mind effectively.

Once he realizes that he has the ability to use his mind effectively, then we can teach him precise, effective strategies for how to learn. When he has effective tools for learning, it dramatically enhances his perception of his own ability to be a successful student, his performance in school, his self-csteem and relationships with friends and family, just to name a few. When a young person understands (for many, for the first time in their lives) that he is intelligent, that he IS a good student, that he CAN learn easily and that there is nothing "wrong" with him, that has a dramatic impact on every aspect of his life! Now we can move on to teaching strategies for mastering thoughts and emotions and taking action on goals.

Play and learning

Play and learning go hand in hand. Children learn much of their life skills such as coping with day-to-day life and primary school pressures, meeting challenges, and making better decisions from participating in outdoor play activities. The purpose of this research is to learn about the significance of integrating outdoor play as support for enhancing creative learning of the children. Play and learning is successful when teachers transfer the skills students learned during their outdoor play activities to the classroom setting and other settings outside the classroom. Synthesized data from related studies will supplement the required content for the discussion. This study seeks to reinforce awareness on the importance of the combination of social and cognitive play categories as part of the outdoor play activities to influence the children's behavior, perception, enthusiasm, and speed of learning. Learning through play is a natural and necessary activity, which teachers can help to maximize.

Play and learning are crucial aspects in children's daily lives because it functions to unfold the knowledge around them. Outdoor play promotes children's healthy physical development and enables children to pick up the necessary skills to meet the challenges of adulthood through their own directed outdoor play. John Dewey supported the concept of theory of experience. The child simultaneously extends command or operation over the object by further exploring its characteristics, weaknesses and strengths. This means that the child is exhibiting and extending personal repertoire of habit, skills, and control of the surrounding - learning - through mere play. Even the simplest toy would mean a lot to a child because he can manipulate a toy and in the process understands the structure involved in learning and handling the toy.

Outdoor play in primary school is linked to children's social and cognitive development, which further strengthens the correlation between play and learning. Through outdoor play and learning learning, children develop self-confidence, independence, and communication skills when socially interacting with others. It is also important in keeping their positive dispositions when they are engage in their learning environment. The constantly changing rules of the games, interactions with different peer groups, and the differing environment of the outdoor play allow children to feel the variations as well as formulate perceptions of their outdoor experience.

The outdoor experience could be the simple variations of temperature, light, movement, color, smell, and texture, which are the fundamentals of being outdoors. These contribute to the emotional and spiritual well being of the children as well as enhance their enthusiasm for social interaction. Children would respond to their environment using the appropriate skills and knowledge. Given a piece of play material that a child has never seen or experienced in his life, the child would definitely explore, play, and learn about the characteristics and features of the toy.

Outdoor play for children usually takes place in designated play areas around the neighborhood where there are places for running and climbing. The availability of play resources, space and toys, are important factors that would contribute to the development of children. An outdoor-play e□uipment research detailing the amount of play resources provided in children's playgrounds concluded that playgrounds with less extensive resources or toys fostered greater deal of social contacts among children. However, the children tend to perform less exercise and experienced as well as developed more social conflicts in obtaining these play and learning materials. The social conflicts between children during playtime were usually caused by competition for material or toy possession. This issue of aggressive play would tend to increase when they reach primary school age.

The children's desire for privacy at play areas also presents a challenge to professionals responsible for designing the play e□uipment and program especially the use of the outdoor play environments. Adults handling children's outdoor play should learn to consider as risk the probability that children would be out of adult's constant gaze because of their tendency to go to private spaces, nooks, and corners of the play e□uipments. Adults need to be responsible enough to learn to balance freedom with risks protection. The adults could exercise responsible flexibility for children to enjoy freedom during outdoor play and learning. Children will always desire a versatile outdoor area where to impose control on their play and learning environment.

CHAPTER 2- HOW DO CHILDREN LEARN

Learning is natural instinct in a child. They enjoy it. It is interesting event and also a motivating subject for the parents to see their child learning. They not only take pleasure from their efforts but also try to improve the process through which a child learns. A careful approach is re□uired when initiating a child for learning.

Parents and teachers always advise the children to learn, but hardly instruct them how to learn. Learning is a natural process. The child him self will learn something through natural process. However, what is important is 'How to learn'.

The child learns through observations. Child always tries to observe what is around him. Learning process starts from this instinct. He uses all his efforts and senses to initiate learning.

Parents should keep in mind that their children do not know any thing about philosophy or theory. They are very practical and would choose learning everything through practice. Hence it is advisable to allow them to learn everything in their own style not according to your style.

When a child comes in this world, his brain has great potential for learning and development. This is gifted from God. As children interact with their environment, they learn problem solving skills, critical thinking skills, and language skills just through observation and competition. Parents need not to interfere in this practice but they need to develop an atmosphere where the child can learn and grow naturally.

Gradually children develop a sense of self and then a sense of belonging to a family. They begin to watch other children and to wish to interact with them. Children learning skill develops through various stages. He may like to play alone, then near others but not with them. Again playing with others but not sharing with them etc. Over the time, he knows the importance of company and learns the ability to respect the feeling and rights of others.

3 Different Ways School Children Learn Material

Children want to succeed just as adults do this includes school work and assignments but all children learn differently.

One way that a child could learn is by watching someone doing it, while explaining it step by step. At first, they may struggle to learn the new skill but once they grasp that information you can be assured that they know it. They have to visually see it being done then usually would like for that person to watch them do it to make sure that they are doing it correctly.

The second way that children learn is by reading it out of a book then applying what they learned and using that information. Some children and adults are not able to do that and would have a difficult learning if that was the only way to do it. This may be one of the hardest ways to learn something new.

The last way that children learn is by trail and error. This is mostly hands on experimental. These children like to be given a project then they would like to be left alone to figure it out for themselves. Many children will try to do something over and over again till they get it right. This can lead to frustration for the children. Many children will give up hope if they can not master it correctly within a few tries.

Not all children will learn the same way it is important to find out which way your child learns best then stick with that way. This is easier to do and accomplish if you are homeschooling your children, where you can take the time to teach them the way that they learn the best.

Home schooling a child that is having difficulty learning in school can excel at home by changing the method of teaching. It does not have to be expensive to home school your child there are many free resources online. You can home school inexpensively.

Simple Educational Activities For Helping Children Learn

Various educational activities may be utilized to help children in the learning process. Children of all ages may utilize these activities. One of the latest and most effective tools of learning happens to be the toys. Children can be made to focus on certain learning areas through these toys. These toys ignite the child's interest and are conducive in the process of learning. These educational toys are the perfect tools to be used in various settings. They at times are specially catered to meet the needs of children faced with learning difficulties.

Books

This is one of the best options for helping children practice the skills of reading and writing. They help children learn skills at all levels. Engaging a child with the image and words of the book will assist in stimulating the senses. This will then aid in all subjects including math, reading and writing.

The process of learning can be made more attractive, appealing, and interesting through various practical activities. Books also help teach sounds which allow the child to interact in certain ways.

Board games

There are many board and card games designed specifically for helping a child learn. These physical games happen to be a great tool for assisting children in leaning the art of counting and numbering. The children may be taught to learn letters and spellings through these games. The focus should always be on teaching the child how to play instead of teaching it to win. These card or board games are a useful source of help that aids the learning process of children of all ages in the form of extra teaching activities.

Toys

Toys can be made into an essential part of activities that will help children learn apart from boosting their self esteem. These typically includes the wooden toys. Activities such as building blocks or something similar using different sizes, shapes and color are helpful in stimulating the senses of a child. It also teaches the children the different colors and counting. These activities also help children with logical thinking.

Computer

The learning process of a child can be improved significantly through laptop or online games. These games regardless of what they are based on will assist the child with a process of learning that is much more engaging and fun. The games are usually based on images, sounds, and words. Such games provide basic and advanced techni ues of learning.

These activities over the past few years have been specifically designed to aid the process of learning among the children of all ages. They are a useful tool that needs to be utilized to assist children in the process of learning. These activities are increasingly becoming a vital part of all educational institutes starting from pre-school till school. This is because teachers and caregivers now acknowledge the importance of these activities. This is why you have these activities as a part of curriculum.

Simpler is better when it comes to early childhood development. With technology taking over all aspects of life including education, books, board games, and toys, still, happen to be the most effective educational activities for kids and teens.

CHAPTER 3- TEACHING READING TO CHILDREN- WHY IS READING TO CHILDREN IMPORTANT

I vividly remember lying in my mother's arms as she read Charlotte's Web to me. The room was ⬜uiet and I was completely transported by my mother's words to another world. She would bring the story alive with different voices, sound effects and exaggerated gestures and we both became deeply involved in the lives of Fern, her pet pig Wilbur and his friend Charlotte, the spi-der. It was a magical experience and one that will stay with me always.

You, too, can probably remember a favorite bedtime story and the warm and secure feelings that time evoked. Children love being read to it is a fact! There is something truly satisfying about becoming wrapped up in the fantasy of the moment. Children are intrigued not only by the story itself but by the sound and rhythm of the language and being read aloud to allows the child to let his imagination run free while in the safety of a parent's arms.

In this time of high-tech computer games, videos and TV, you may wonder if you are fighting a losing battle when it comes to reading. Long gone are the days when families would sit around listening intently to mothers or fathers reading aloud. There are so many different forms of entertainment today that it is difficult to know how to get the balance right.

But books are special. Not only do they play a vital role in language development but they can also entertain, teach and inform. They can stimulate your child's fertile imagination and even help him to come to terms with the pains and pleasures of growing up. Sometimes reading about someone else's life experience can help the reader deal with his own problems.

Books are enriching in so many ways and children should be read aloud to and encouraged to read for themselves as much as possible without it being a chore. It is up to you to make reading fun; after all, children love and need to laugh and so do parents! A good giggle at bedtime can really help alleviate the stresses and strains of the day.

Reading books together is a special experience and one that will continue for years to come. Many children adore being read to right up to their teens and as a parent you should try and enjoy this unique closeness for as long as you can. The more you share the experience together, the more your child will love books and eventually reading for himself.

By reading aloud to your child, you are introducing him to a lifelong pleasure.

Why is Reading to Children Important?

Growing up, my parents read a story to me every night. I always assumed it was the standard in every child's bedtime routine across the country. As a teacher with my degree in Early Childhood Education, I know the importance of reading to children. The benefits associated with a simple daily bedtime story seem endless. Imagine my amazement when I read the statistic stating that only 39% of parents read to their children on a daily basis (Young, Davis, and Schoen, 1996).

In a word, I was flabbergasted. I've witnessed the struggling readers and the impact that has on their daily lives. When a child has difficulties reading, everything in school suffers as a result. Would something as simple as a daily ten minute bedtime story interaction between a parent and child prevent these kids from struggling throughout their school years? Could it really be that simple? I want parents to know how vital it is to read to their children everyday.

Teaches Basic Reading and Writing Skills

When children are being read to, they are taking in so much at once. Simple things experienced readers may take for granted are introduced during the first few years of life while listening to a story. Children who are familiar with books know how to hold a book and turn the pages from left to right. They know that the book has a title.

Pre-readers also understand that the book contains pictures and words and they start distinguishing words and letters. They begin to recognize that the printed text is read from right to left and top to bottom, which is directly related to beginning writing skills. School districts expect children to be reading simple word texts by the end of kindergarten, and having these basic skills can propel them toward success.

Teaches Basic Listening Skills

It's true, as I experience it in the classroom everyday. Some children don't have the ability to sit still long enough to listen to a story. It can be possible that some children may have trouble because of a disability, but others may simply lack the insight to what story time is all about. Making story time at home a daily, fun and engaging activity can encourage children to get excited about story time at school which can also discourage behavior issues.

Promotes Vocabulary and Language Skills

Just think of all the new words children hear from books. Our daily conversations do not require much use of complex language or vocabulary and can hinder the development of a child's oral language. Reading to a child can introduce so many new words, especially nonfiction titles. Children's literature provides great models of language for children. In hearing the flow of the writing and the innovative words, especially in repeated readings of the same text, can nurture children's language development.

Builds Knowledge of the World

As in language development, reading exposes children to worlds of new information. As a teacher, I used books to teach children about a topic, such as a place, or a person, or a topic. The amount of information a child can learn from books is never-ending, which leads into the next benefit.

Fosters a Love of Reading

Enabling children to enjoy reading is one of the most important gifts a parent can do. Kids will learn reading skills in school, but they will come to associate reading with work, not pleasure. As a result, they may lose their desire to read, effecting their schoolwork and desire to learn. When a parent shares an exciting story with a child, and in turn, gets excited with the child, the parent is showing how much fun reading can be. Jim Trelease, author of The Read-Aloud Handbook, encourages parents to lead by example by stating; "Make sure your children see you reading for pleasure other than at read-aloud time. Share with them your enthusiasm for whatever you are reading".

Encourages Parent-Child Bonding

Reading aloud also creates special time for parents to bond with their children. Cuddling together for a bedtime story, you'll be helping your children develop a lifelong appreciation for reading. (Reading Aloud, n.d.) Builds Self-Esteem Children often want to hear the same story over and over. Just as adults may need to hear something more than once to remember or understand, children are the same way.

CHAPTER 4- HOW TO TEACH CHILDREN READING

Teaching reading to children can be a lot of fun, as children love to learn. They can see you reading and they want to be able to read also. Children love stories, when they are growing up they make up stories in their fantasy world all the time. So when you are teaching reading to children start by reading in bed.

Let your children pick the books they want to hear. Read aloud and as you are reading always underline the words you are reading with your finger or a pencil so your children know word makes what sound. Also children love playing games so when I am teaching reading to children I use the Montessori approach.

This is a combination of phonics and sandpaper letters. Phonics are a must when you are teaching reading to children so they join the spoken sounds with the written word. They are the code to unlock what the words sound like. When your child can read the word the same way as the word is spoken then they will know what the word is.

Sandpaper letters come in handy because as your child traces the words written with the sandpaper letters she also speaks it. This helps to plant the phonic sounds and phonic combinations in your child's brain.

A problem that does arise with phonics is when the child is saying the new word using phonics they speak the word too slowly. You must tell them to say the word faster so it actually sounds like the spoken word. When they can hear the word spoken then they should know the meaning if they have already learnt the word.

Developing a genuine love for reading in children- advice for teachers and parents

Many children today are so engrossed in the latest technology that they barely have time to open a book and read. As teachers, we have to help them develop a genuine love for reading at an early age.

So how exactly do we do this? Well it doesn't take a genius to do so. Here are some very easy and practical ways on how you can make your pupils love reading:

• Be a role model

Children learn best through modeling. Have you noticed how children would often emulate the way you act or talk? In fact, there are times they even play teacher and you'll be surprised to see them copy the way you move and talk to them in class. So you can just imagine the extent of your influence among these young learners.

If you want your children to love reading you have to show them that you also love it. Read a book in front of your class every now and then especially during break time or after school hours. Show them your collection of books and let them see you enjoy reading them.

• Use varied reading materials

Children are easily bored especially if they're always reading the same textbook. You should not only develop a love for reading in your pupils but also teach them to appreciate all kinds of reading materials. Let them go to the library once in a while where they can read encyclopedias, almanacs, journals, fairytales, legends, and so much more.

• Provide wholesome reading activities

Many children are not fond of reading because afterwards teachers/parents would only ask them questions then that's it. Teachers/parents often fail to provide enrichment activities. As a guadian, you must be resourceful enough to come up with some wholesome activities in line with reading. For instance, if the children read a fairytale you can ask them to act out or draw their favorite parts.

Integrate reading in all your lessons. Allow them to read even if it's not their English class. You can let them read the procedure in their experiments in Science or the instructions in their arts and crafts activities. You should also give assignments that include reading a variety of resources from magazines to online references. In other words, you should make reading a part of your everyday lessons. Once you're able to do all these, it won't be long before your children develop a genuine love for reading.

Parenting Tips - Finding Out the Right Time to Start Teaching Your Child How to Read

One of the things that every parent should know is the reality that their baby's brain is swiftly developing. This explains why many parents take advantage of this period prompting them to feed intelligent information in the simplest way possible. This is due to the fact that the wiring of the brain and the development of all its areas happens until the first five years of his or her life. During birth, the brain of a neonate can be just like a blank space waiting to be filled up with intelligible things, of course. One of the best parenting tips that one should be aware of is that each opportunity that you provide your kid with has a possible effect in how they will live their life. This is because learning is a second nature to young babies.

This is why stimulation is advised by your baby's pediatrician because learning is what they are born to do.

Lessons about parenting tips would instruct you to provide each and every opportunity for your kid to learn. Five years is a short period considering the plenty of things that babies are capable to discover and learn about, isn't it? If you carefully observe their actions, it would seem like they know about the short span of time that is allotted for them to learn more about the world around them making them too curious to touch, taste, see, hear and know everything that they notice around them.

Now, many parents especially mothers have become too particular with teaching their kids to read at the earliest time possible. They seem to be so enthusiastic to teach reading while their babies are still in their infancy period. While it is true that you can begin teaching reading to as early as three months old, it is still vital to put into consideration some things that would provide hints that your baby is reading to start on with reading lessons. This is to prevent pushing them too much because every baby is different in their own skills and capabilities.

One of the simplest activities that you can carry out if you want to be sure if your baby is now ready to begin a reading program is to look into their visual tracking skills. You can do this by basically holding an object approximately 9 inches away from their face. If you notice that your kid can follow the object through their eyes if you move it from left to right or up and down, then you can begin to teach your baby how to read.

To make your kid be more interested and enthusiastic with the reading program, it would be ideal to use colorful books that can attract his attention. As you teach him or her, try to pay attention to what excites your baby based on his reactions.

But if you expect that your baby would immediately demonstrate what he or she might have learned from your reading sessions, of course, he won't during the early months of the program. When you start it during the early three months of life, for sure, it would not be possible to hear a three-year old baby reading his books that is not what this book is trying to imply. It may take a year before your baby can show the reading ability that he has learned from your reading lessons.

Parenting involves a lot of responsibilities starting from the day that you gave birth to your child. Be resourceful and you are sure to get to what you are aiming for when it comes to helping your kid how to read.

Improving their reading pace

Parents often ask me how they can help their child improve their reading pace. Parents know that reading is the key to succeeding in school for their student, and more importantly it is the key to succeeding in today's knowledge-driven world. With information doubling every six months, reading faster is no longer a luxury. It is a necessity. This section will provide the answer you need to help your child read faster.

The best way to increase a child's reading pace is by having them practice reading. Like any other skill, the more you perform it, the better you get a doing it.

Some of the real problem for many parents is getting their child interested in reading. Let's look at the reason why many children do not like to read.

Today's child is used to playing video games, watching television, and going to the movies. The information they see in each of this situations is changing very rapidly. When they begin to read a book, the pace of the information slows down dramatically. That is because when you read, there is a little voice in back of your brain that pronounces each word slowly. This slow reading speed is so boring that many children simply refuse to read. Fortunately, there is a simple solution.

Getting your child to read more so they can improve their reading pace is incredibly easy. First, determine what your child really enjoys. For example, my son, loved to play video games when he was younger. He hated to read. The solution was simple. I purchased a subscription to a video game magazine. Each month, he would wait for his magazine to arrive, and would devour every page as soon as it came. He became the best video game player in his school. His reading speed also improved. Today, my son is an adult. He still loves to read, but his taste in reading materials has matured. Here's how to apply this to your child.

Find their passion. Determine what publications cater to that passion. For example, does your son love sports? Get him a "Sports Illustrative," subscription. Does your daughter love fashion? Get her a subscription to "17 Magazine." Once you give your child reading material they actually desire to learn, they will begin reading more. As they read more they will evolve higher reading speeds. Everyone wins.

CHAPTER 5- SKILLS AND READING COMPREHENSION

What Is Reading Comprehension?

Reading comprehension can simply be defined as understanding what you are reading. Even though that sounds easy it really isn't, because it re uires our full attention and focus when reading. If you aren't properly processing what you are reading as you are reading through text then you have poor reading comprehension, and if you do then vice-versa. Its pretty much impossible to try and captivate the act of comprehending, but that's why improving your comprehension is a process.

Essentially reading comprehension works by series of cognitive processes. When a person begins to read, the brain is using its understanding of individual sounds in language, phonics (connection between letters and sounds and the relationship between sounds, letters, and words) and the ability to construct a meaning from what you are reading, which is the essentially the end result: comprehension.

There are elements that make up the techni ue of reading comprehension: vocabulary knowledge & text comprehension. In order to understand what you're reading you must be able to understand the vocabulary used in the piece of writing you're reading. If the individual words have no meaning then the general story won't either. Children can use what they know about vocabulary to try and process it, but they also re uire to continually be taught new words. Aside from understanding each word in a text, a child also has to be able to make sense of them and has to be able to come up with a conclusion of what it truly means, this process overall is referred to as text comprehension. It's much more complex and varied than just basic vocabulary knowledge. Readers applies □uite a few different text comprehension strategies to enhance reading comprehension. These include surveillance for understanding, answering, and developing □uestions, summarizing & being aware of and using a text's construction to aid comprehension.

Without comprehension, reading is simply like keeping track of symbols on a page with your eyes & sounding them out. Think about being presented with a story written in Egyptian hieroglyphics with no understanding of their significance. You may value the words visually then be able to come up with various small pieces of meaning from the page, but you are not really reading through the story. The letters on the page do not possess a meaning. They are really simply symbols. People read for many purposes, however, understanding is invariably an integral part of their objective. Reading comprehension is essential simply because without it reading doesn't provide the reader with any specific information.

Reading comprehension is truly crucial to existence. Much continues to be written about the importance of practical literacy. In order to endure and thrive in today's world individuals will have to be able to comprehend common texts such as bills, mortgage agreements (leases, purchase contracts), instructions on packaging and travel documents (bus and train schedules, maps, travel directions). Reading comprehension is a vital component of functional literacy. Consider the potentially dire conse□uences of not having the ability to comprehend dosage directions on a bottle of medicine or even warnings on a container of dangerous chemicals. With the ability to understand whatever they read, individuals are able not only to live securely and efficiently, but additionally to continue to develop socially, emotionally and intellectually.

Now, the big question is, how do children comprehend what read?

Reading comprehension in children

Probably the single most important aspect of your child's early academic development is learning to read and acquiring and sustaining a love of reading. Of course any child's interest needs to be perked in order for them to want to read and read and read and slowly progress from simple books with large illustrations and words to longer books with fewer illustrations and smaller words. The journey to a love of reading is rarely accomplished overnight, but once you have reached that destination, a whole new world will open up for your child where he or she can visit places only dreamed about, live in that beautiful castle, become friends with the fairies and take a safari trip to Africa, perhaps even journey to the centre of the earth!

At the end of each story I research, there are notes for discussion and comprehension questions. I feel it important to place the learners in various groups depending on their reading abilities and exposure to phonics and phonic awareness. I have no doubt that most children will require some assistance in understanding the ☐uestions. This is where I encourage fun interaction between educator and learner.

It may be so that answers will have be recorded by the educator manually and suggestions made by the educator. These subtle reading comprehension exercises will go far to show an educator in a year or less how far a child has progressed and where his or her interests lie and to enhance and encourage a love of reading.

Positive interaction between educator and child is imperative and will make this a fun learning experience as he or she watches you do your "homework". Who said homeschooling isn't hands on?

You will be able to decide which ☐uestions and discussion points are appropriate for your child. The purpose of these exercises is to establish the understanding of the story and the concept and to enhance concentration, listening and reading skills.

I cannot stress enough the importance of allowing a child to develop at his or her own pace. There is no need to progress to a more advanced book, no matter how short, until educator and the child are quite confident that he or she has grasped the first story and that he or she is ☐uite comfortable with the discussion and ☐uestions that are an integral part of reading comprehension activities.

When Children Read Well, Yet Lack Comprehension

A common reading disorder goes undiagnosed until it becomes problematic, according to the results of a five-year study published online in the journal "Brain Connectivity".

Dyslexia, a reading disorder in which a child confuses letters and struggles with sounding out words, has been the focus of much research into reading. That is not the case, however, with the lesser known disorder Specific Reading Comprehension Deficits or S-RCD, in which a child reads successfully but does not sufficiently comprehend the meaning of the words.

According to lead investigator Laurie Cutting at Vanderbilt's Peabody College of Education and Human development, a person with S-RCD will explain it like this: "I can read Spanish, because I know what sounds the letters make and how the words are pronounced, but I couldn't tell you what the words actually mean."

"When a child is a good reader, it's assumed their comprehension is on track. But three to ten percent of those children don't understand most of what they're reading. By the time the problem is recognized, often closer to third or fourth grade, the disorder is disrupting their learning process," Cutting said.

Researchers have been able to pinpoint brain activity and understand its role in dyslexia, but no functional magnetic resonance imaging or fMRI studies, until now, have examined the neurobiological profile of those who exhibit poor reading comprehension despite intact word-level abilities.

Neuro-imaging of children showed that, while reading, the brain function of those with S-RCD is quite different and distinct from those with dyslexia. Those with dyslexia exhibited abnormalities in a specific region in the occipital-temporal cortex, a part of the brain that is associated with successfully recognizing words on a page. Those with S-RCD, on the other hand, did not show abnormalities in this region, instead showing specific abnormalities in regions typically associated with memory.

That there will be defects in the brain areas concerned with memory makes sense. Several studies have confirmed that reading comprehension relies heavily upon both working memory and long-term memory.

Short-term memory holds information in the mind for only a few seconds while it is being processed. Long-term memory is where such processed information is permanently stored. Working memory is an intermediary and active memory system in the information processing area of the brain. It is an important memory system and one that most of us use every day.

Sentence comprehension depends heavily upon adequate working memory. For example, working memory is required to comprehend sentences that are complex in structure such as, "The clown that is hugging the boy is kissing the girl." It helps us interpret sentences that are lengthy, "Do every other problem on page fifteen and all of the problems on page sixteen before checking your answers in the back of the book." We use working memory when preservation of word order (syntax) is important to correctly understand a sentence like; "It was the boy's ball and not the girl's that was dirty."

The good news is that weaknesses in cognitive skills can be attacked head-on. The key is to identify the specific weaknesses, such as a poor working memory, and to strengthen these mental skills through training and practice.

If you suspect that your child has a cognitive deficiency, get appropriate help as soon as possible. The gap between children with and those without cognitive deficits gets wider and wider and may become more difficult, and later impossible to close.

Helping your child with reading comprehension

What are some things you as a parent can do to help your children improve their reading and reading comprehension skills?

Encourage your child to spend some time each day reading. It is important for you to be a good role model. Your children need to see that reading is important to you and that you enjoy reading. They need to observe that you value reading, that it is a daily habit for you and you need to talk about how reading helps you everyday, including at your place of employment.

Talk about what you are reading to your children. Point out articles in newspapers and magazines that you have read which they may find interesting. Tell them the storyline of the latest book you are reading. Ask them questions about the materials they are reading. Show a real interest in what they are reading.

"A room without a book is like a body without a soul". You may not agree with the ancient orator Cicero who said that, but having lots of books around your home is very important. There should always be something for kids to read. Check books out of the public library. Find out about authors your child enjoys and order more books by that writer. There are many great magazines for kids.

In order to improve listening comprehension it is important to talk with children about movies and television programs they watch and books and stories you have read aloud to them. See how much of the material they have heard they can remember. Here are some kinds of questions to ask children to answer after they have read or heard a story or book or watched a movie or television program.

*Who were the main characters? What did you find out about them? How are the characters like you? Which character was most like you? How are you different than the characters? If you got to play the part of one of the characters in the movie which one would you pick and why?

*What is the setting? Where did this story take place? Did it take place in the past, present or future? How do you know?

*What questions do you have after reading this story or watching this movie?

* Now that the book or movie is over what do you predict will happen next to the characters? If there was a sequel to this book or movie what would it be about? If you could change the ending what would you have happen instead of what happened in the book or movie?

* Can we learn any lessons from this television program? What does this book teach us? What message do you think the movie director wanted to get across to people?

*What was the mood? Was it scary? Did it make you sad? Was it a tragedy or a comedy?

*What would you change about this movie or book? What was your favorite part? What was the worst part? Why did you like it? Why didn't you like it? If you had to give this movie or book a rating out of 10 what would you give it and why?

*Every good story has a problem that needs to be solved. What was the problem in this book, movie or television program? How did it get solved?

*See if you can describe the beginning, middle and end of this story in a few sentences.

* What kind of story was this? Science fiction? Mystery? Adventure? Biography? Historical Fiction?

* Do you think this story was fiction or non-fiction? Why do you think that?

If you can, spend time every day reading aloud to your children. The great American poet Robert Frost once said, "You can't read a word you've never heard." Children needs to hear the beauty of language from adults who love and care about them. This fosters not only family togetherness but a love of literature and an appreciation of the power of language.

What are reading instructions

What if there was one simple thing you could do to ensure your child would read well and enjoy reading?

What if that thing didn't cost a penny?

Would you be interested?

Of course, you would. Here it is. The one thing you can do to improve your child's reading and reading comprehension is to significantly increase the amount of speaking and listening.

That's it.

Too simple, you say? Nope, research shows those children who are read to aloud and talked to learn patterns of language and meaning that they recall when they read. In fact, what they do is mirror back the language onto the printed word.

It works like this. A child learns a word and its meaning by hearing it, that is they experience the word. When they learn to read, they draw on that meaning or experience. If the child has a deficit in oral language experiences, he will have less to bring to reading. The word doesn't make sense to him because he has not sensed (experienced) it.

The richer the oral language experience, the □uicker and better the child reads. Researchers call oral language experiences orality. So, just as literacy is the ability to read and write, orality is the ability to speak and listen.

Here's a big surprise. The most important aspect of children's language experience is its amount. Betty Hart and Todd R. Risley, authors of Meaningful Differences in the Everyday Experiences of Young American Children did a longitudinal study in which they recorded each month, for 2-1/2 years, one full hour of every word spoken at home between parent and child in 42 families, categorized as professional, working class, or welfare families.

By age three the vocabulary of the children from professional families was dramatically higher by several hundred words than that of child in a family on welfare. Hart and Risely estimate that in a year a 3-year-old from a professional family will hear 11 million words, while a child from a welfare family will hear only 3 million.

What are the implications? Staggering, if you imagine that orality is the key to a lasting literacy. These authors checked in on the children again at age nine. They found profound differences in the level of learning, literacy and social maturity.

What kind of oral language experiences are best? Ordering or demanding certain behaviors of your child isn't the kind of orality we mean. The best kinds of experiences include genuine sharing and dialogue.

Here are a few: Reading aloud high-□uality literature (this is a must every day) Nursery rhymes and fairy tales Word games, like tongue twisters and silly sayings Telling stories you make up Enjoying a magazine together, where you ask your child to tell you about the pictures.

Other ways are: Use open-ended questions rather than making statements. (E.g. that's a beautiful picture you drew, can you tell me about it?) Talk about the process of doing something while doing it. (E.g. when going to the store or cooking or repairing talk to your child about what you are doing). Any activity which allows your child to both speak and listen.

Remember, it's the simple things in life, like talking and listening to your child-- that make the difference. In this case, the difference lasts a lifetime.

Crucial Areas In Reading Instruction- Important note for both parents and teachers

The most crucial areas in reading today are parental involvement and the home environment in a child's literacy development. I can look at the importance of the home environment from the standpoint of both a parent and an educator. As a parent, I can relate to the time constraints, financial responsibilities, and stress that raising children can place on a person. It was often frustrating not being informed of my children's progress in school until a problem arose. The problem could have been averted had I been notified far enough in advance.

Communication is essential in curtailing areas of misconception that may become major problems at a later date. As an educator, I would like to offer direction to help parents become involved in assisting their children to succeed through open communication so that perceptual differences do not become major problems.

I am very concerned because I hear many teachers complain that parents don't care. At the same time, parents expect the school system to solve the social and behavioral problems for which they should be responsible. It seems that teachers blame parents and parents blame teachers for what appears to be a lack of standards, accountability, and responsibility for today's children. Instead of pointing the finger at one another, it is time that both educators and parents become sincerely involved as a team to encourage and support early childhood literacy development. Many parents want to be actively involved in their child's literacy efforts, but they feel intimidated by the frightening monolith; called the school system. In many economically deprived families the power of knowledge in others makes them feel inadequate, while negative appraisals of their children by teachers, becomes a negative comment about their lives.

I had the opportunity to work with an urban male high school student. His mother refused to come to school for the parent teacher conference because she said that she felt uncomfortable. When I asked her why she felt uncomfortable she said school was "too big". She was reticent to discuss the issue further. I explained to her that I am a parent too and realized how stressful it can be at times. She related to the fact that we were both parents, at which point she seemed open to suggestions as to how we could work together to help her son. She still did not want to come to school, but became comfortable having telephone discussions with me as to how we could improve her son's literacy. She said that no one ever asked for her input when it came to her son's education. I think an early childhood literacy program would have helped the family significantly because the mother sincerely cared about her son's education.

Some parents do not feel competent to deal with school work. This phenomenon may reflect parents insecurity in the school setting or fears about participation in their children's learning.

Some teachers have negative attitudes about parents and parent participation, sometimes claiming that parents are apathetic and come to school only to criticize. Teachers should not assume that parents are not willing to help with their children's education. Many parents are willing to help with their children's education but may have few ideas about how to provide this help.

There are several things parents can do at home to help in their child's literacy development. One of the areas where parents can help children to become literate, I call survival reading. For example, there are many situations at home to provide practice for interpreting product information. Learning to read labels and interpreting the information is a necessity. If there is a tube of preparation H and a tube of Crest toothpaste on the bathroom sink, it is obviously important to know the difference. It is equally important to note warnings on labels as well as being able to read nutritional information on cans and boxes of food. Children can help make out grocery lists, balance checkbooks, write messages on greeting cards, and read recipes.

We all need to be more positive in our communication with one another. Teachers need to talk with parents, and parents need to talk with teachers in a nonthreatening nonconfrontational manner. Communication is the key to building a better understanding and support of literacy programs. I feel very strongly that a sound educational system needs parents, teachers, and community. Helping parents understand how children become readers and writers is one of the teachers and the school administrators most important missions.

Some parents are illiterate or low-literate. These parents can guide their children at home with skills such as cooking, critically watching television, going to the library and getting books on tape. If teachers have ascertained that these activities exist in the homes of some of their children, they could point out to the parents the value of increased attention to the print embedded in these activities.

Emergent literacy opportunities have nothing to do with socioeconomic status. It is family literacy practices mentioned above which determine young children experiences with print in the home. Parents need to be viewed as participants in their childrens learning, then teachers need to implement initiatives that bring schools and communities closer together.

CHAPTER 6- TEACHING CHILDREN READING METHODS

The two most widely used teaching methods for reading are the phonics method and the total reading method (whole language). There have been decades of acrimonious debate in the teaching community over which method is best -- the so-called 'reading war'. The proponents of both methods extol the benefits of their system and decry the weaknesses of the other.

At times, the debate has become bitter and personal, raising strong passions from both sides. The die-hards in both camps can be very entrenched in their beliefs. It is good to know they are so passionate about the education of our children, although sometimes it seems like they just want to be right.

In truth, there are positive and negative aspects to both methods.

Total Reading / Whole Language

The total reading method, also known as whole language, is how most adults read. We look at the whole word and we know it. We do not need to phonetically sound out the word in our heads because we have seen it hundreds of times before and we recognize it.

The system's proponents say that since this is how most adults read, it makes sense that children should learn the same way. They say that children will naturally learn the phonetic rules as their reading vocabulary increases. Children are taught to recognize whole words rather than individual sounds. This method gives children ⬜uick access to reading skills, which encourages them to progress.

This method is often taught with picture books or flashcards. Simple clear pictures help the child associate the word.

The problem with total reading is the child cannot read new words. If the child does not know the word, she does not have the phonetic skills to put the letter sounds together and deduce the word. The supporters of total reading claim children will learn the phonetic rules naturally. The supporters of the phonics method highly dispute that claim.

Phonics

In the phonics teaching system, the child learns the phonetic rules that form words. They learn the letters of the alphabet and the sounds they make. They then learn to blend the sounds together to form simple words; at, in, on, etc. They then advance to three and four letter words until eventually they can form complex words.

The system's proponents say that learning phonics is the essential basis of reading. Children will naturally drift to scan reading (total reading) as they become older but they will always need the phonics base so they can read new words. Phonics also allows students to make educated guesses at how to spell new words.

There are two main problems with the phonics teaching method. The first is that it can be rather boring for the children. Learning the letters of the alphabet and their associated sounds is a slow and tedious exercise. This is very much down to the ability of the teacher.

The big problem with phonics is that the English language has so many inconsistencies that it just does not work. How do you teach a child phonics but also explain that words as simple as 'do' and 'go' do not rhyme.

How do you explain that 'cow' and 'how' do not rhyme with 'low' and 'mow' (which do rhyme with 'go'). How do you explain that the 'g' sound in words like 'gem', 'gel', 'giant' and 'giraffe' does not sound the same as in words like 'get', 'gibbon', 'gift' and 'girl'. There are no phonetic rules to explain these inconsistencies and the English language is packed with them. You just have to know the words.

To teach the phonics method you need books that use regular words that are phonetically consistent. You introduce all the inconsistencies later.

Which Method to Use?

So which method is the better method for a child? There does not appear to be a right or wrong answer. Children who learn better visually will probably benefit more from the whole language method. Children who are auditory learners may benefit more from the phonics method. But a more reasonable and beneficial approach may be not to choose one method over the other at all, but to instead blend both methods so that children can learn how words are put together, and still comprehend the text that they are reading. After all, it is the ability to understand what is read that opens up a child's world through reading.

The debate over which method is best continues. Fortunately, common sense has mostly prevailed over teaching dogma. As mentioned above, the majority of the world's English teaching community has now come to accept that what they need is a combination of both teaching methods. Students gain a more rounded and solid reading skills base by learning to read with a mixture of both methods. It allows students to develop a complete set of reading skills without the gaps left by learning from a single method. It also helps teachers and parents to keep their lessons varied and entertaining for their students.

Teaching Children Through Stories

Looking at the countless programs and methods available in the child education market, you may feel like you need a Ph.D. in this area if you are to succeed. Then there are the other excuses too like "I have to work and don't have the time," or "I don't have the patience."

Well, here is your wake up call. Teaching can be simple, effective and doable. Reading to your children and using stories to teach is a technique that is within the capabilities of everyone. When we read to our children, we do not confine them to academic excellence but also extend into their emotional and behavioral learning.

The following are 5 reasons why using stories to teach is crucial:

1.The child doesn't feel threatened. It's not another lecture.

When we read to our children, we are able to address a situation in a non-threatening way. What do I mean by threatening? Let's take a look at some examples of habitual phrases we tend to use when "teaching our lesson":

"You shouldn't lie."

"You are so messy."

"You shouldn't be scared. You are just being silly."

"You are not listening to me."

Usually this is done in a blaming or angry tone of voice. When we finger point and use the word "you", children hear negative and the situation becomes tense. Some may even become defensive. Put yourselves in their shoes. If someone were to start attacking you with words, would you be in a teachable mood? I would think not. Rather than focusing on the solutions to the problems, children are focusing on their feelings of anger, hurt, fear etc... that they are experiencing at that moment.

Using stories to teach, we take out the blame and place less emphasis on the problem. We talk and discuss solutions and speak positively. So instead of a lecture, we now have a healthy discussion.

2. Working on "prevention" and "cure".

When we use stories to teach, we can help our children work through situations they are currently experiencing. It also allows us to mentally prepare them for situations that may arise. Children gain experience vicariously through the stories we read. Children are able to learn from vicarious experience just as well as they learn from real ones. The only difference is that this kind of learning takes place in the safety of your home. For example, you could use a book about being bullied to teach your child what to do if and when they face such a situation.

3. The child has a model to follow. They identify with the characters in the book.

Children make connections with the characters of the stories you relate. You can help them further by asking ☐uestions such as:

Is there anyone in the book who reminds you of yourself?

How is that character like you?

Which character would you like to be?

Why would you want to be that character?

Relate the lesson to their own lives and experiences: Like the little pig who build a house of bricks (in the story of the Three Little Pigs), what would you do to make your house strong?

After reading the story of The Little Engine That Could, my daughter began to identify herself with the Little Blue Engine who said "I think I can, I think I can, I think I can." It served to be a good model for her to follow at times when she felt inadequate.

4.Children remember stories better than they remember reprimands. It's a good way to catch their attention.

In Making Connections: Teaching and the Human Brain (Addison-Wesley, 1994), Renate and Geoffery Caine states, "There is strong reason to believe that organization of information in story form is a natural brain process... In a nutshell, neuroscience is discovering that the brain is wired to organize, retain and access information through story. If that is true, then teaching through story means that students will be able to remember what is taught, access that information, and apply it more readily."

Maybe this is why children can rattle off dialogs from their favorite shows but can't remember what mom said about picking up their toys.

5.Allows for critical thinking.

Stories are a safe way for children to explore emotions and behaviors. A book like Jane Simmons' Come Along, Daisy, encourages children to think about the importance of keeping close to parents when out and about . Use thought provoking questions that will lead them to identify problems and feelings such as "How did Daisy get separated from her mother?" and "What was Daisy feeling when she found her mother missing?"

The best kind of teaching you can employ is to teach our children to be authors of solutions. Ask leading questions that will underscore the point of the story such as "How can Daisy avoid getting lost in the future?" What a boost it will be to your children to know they can come up with such genius solutions.

Reading and sharing stories with your children can help you become a better parent. It opens the channel of communication and strengthens the parent-child bond. The magic of stories can be a powerful influence for good. Does that magic exist in your home? Start reading to your child today.

Why is story telling so effective?

Response - Children respond well to stories. They hold children's interest and capture their imagination. Children do not feel they are being dictated to but part of an interactive learning process that you and your child engage in together.

Relaxation - Listening to a story is a calm and relaxing exercise. The child is able to soak up what they are hearing because there is no pressure. They are in an open and responsive state.

Experience - Children can relate to the experiences they hear about in the stories and can put them into a context. This has the advantage of making understanding very accessible for the child. They can identify with the characters and you can discuss this with them.

Memory - Children are much more likely to remember something if they can relate and identify with it. Stories are very memorable to children.

Intelligence - Stories promote critical thinking which can advance a child's intelligence. You can ask them questions that will provoke intelligent thought and lead to discursive thinking that will help enable the child to think for themselves.

Vocabulary - Stories are a great way for children to pick up new words and expand their vocabulary. As your child advances you can increase the level of difficulty of the stories you read them so they are always being challenged and progressing.

Behaviour - Stories offer an excellent opportunity to teach a child the correct way to behave in a given event or situation. Stories can offer positive role models and give good examples of how one should behave.

Speed Reading Techniques For children

To successfully teach your child to speed read, the child should be between eight and twelve years old.

Be sure your child can commit at least fifteen minutes a day to practice the new techniques.

Go the library and get books that are appropriate for the child's age, preferably books the child has not read before.

Choose an appropriate 'reward' system. The type of reward is up to you. It might be your child's favorite snack, an afternoon at the movies, a trip to the toy store or a play date with a friend.

I would suggest keeping it simple and inexpensive.

A box of cookies or candy that can be distributed as appropriate might be more practical than something expensive or time consuming.

You will also need a timer or a watch with a second hand, to track speed reading sessions.

If you can convince a group of neighborhood parents to participate, so much the better.

A group of four to eight children is a great size and the kids will be more likely to practice if they are all participating in the same activity.

The younger the child, the shorter the working sessions should be.

For children of either or nine years of age, keep the sessions around thirty to forty-five minutes.

If the child or group of children begins to get restless and inattentive, stop the session and schedule it for another time.

For children ten to twelve, you can schedule an hour of work and practice.

1. In the first session, explain to the children what you want to accomplish and be sure that they understand that reading will be more fun and rewarding if they use the new techniques.

Have them focus on a dog or a plant in your house or look out the window and find an item to focus on, and then point out how we normally 'see' things.

We don't look at the individual pieces of the item. For example, if we are looking at the house next door, we are seeing the entire house, not the curtain in the front window.

Tell the child that you want them to read in the same way, not by looking at a word on a page, but by looking at a sentence or phrase and seeing the whole concept.

Ask the child to look at a page in a book for five to ten seconds.

Tell them not to try to read the page right now, but just to 'see' the words with a wider lens, to get a broader view of the words on the page, instead of focusing on one or two words.

At the end of this timed exercise, ask them to choose another spot on a different page and do the same thing - this time for ten to twenty seconds.

2. Next, ask them to spend thirty to sixty seconds looking at ten pages of text. But, this time, ask them to 'see' the words with a wider perspective AND try to scan them for meaning at the same time.

At the end of the timed session, ask them to report what they remember. You will be surprised at how much they pick up, even though they aren't reading word-for-word.

Make sure you create a 'fun' environment for the child or children so they don't feel as if they are being tested.

Encourage them by telling them it is OK not to remember much on the first few tries.

When the child does remember something, be sure to praise the newly ac□uired skill.

You may want to offer the reward at this point to keep the children motivated. Even if they only remember one small thing, that is enough to warrant a prize.

Don't dwell on the 'report' section for more than two to four minutes. Just have them quickly tell you what they remember.

Be sure you don't embarrass the child or single them out, whether they remember or not.

As your child gets more comfortable with this wider view of the printed page, they can move on to the next exercise.

3. At this point, you'll want to introduce the visualization aspect to get them more focused and involved in the words on the page.

Have them imagine or visualize what is happening in the book.

As they read a page of text, have them imagine the scene in their head and then tell you about it when they are finished.

Time this exercise for one or two minutes and when the session is finished, ask each child to tell you what they remember and what they 'saw' as they read.

Have the child or children practice this visualization exercise several times until they are more comfortable with the process.

Since most children have a well-developed imagination, it should be easy for them to grasp this technique.

Once you feel the child has mastered visualization, move back to the exercise to 'widen' the scope of their reading window and to increase their speed.

4. Give the child the same instruction, and encourage them to 'see' the wider picture, scanning the pages quickly.

This time, increase the number of pages to fifteen pages in a thirty to sixty second period.

Time this session again and at the end of the session, spend two to four minutes talking about what the child remembers from their reading.

Congratulate them on their progress and offer a reward!

Repeat this session several times, to see if page count and retention improve. Each time, give the child two to four minutes to tell you what they remember.

And provide some positive reinforcement, so that they will want to continue!

5. The next exercise is designed to help the child 'chunk' concepts and information.

Again, have your child select ten to fifteen pages in a book and set the timer for two minutes.

As the child scans the pages using their new technique of 'seeing' with a wider lens, you will signal them with a sound after every five seconds of scanning. Try to use a sound that is not startling or intrusive. A tap with your knuckle or a pen on the edge of the table is fine.

Just don't distract them from their scanning exercise.

At the end of the two minutes, ask the child to briefly tell you what they remembered about what they read and point out any changes you notice in how much they remember or the type of information they remembered during this exercise.

In other words, did the signaling of smaller chunks of time and information change the way they read or how much they saw and remembered?

Repeat this exercise several times before you move on.

After several practice sessions using the 'wide lens' scanning technique and the visualization exercise, you can move on to the next challenge.

6. Now it is time to raise the bar. Tell your child or children that you will give them a special reward if they can finish a short book - twenty to fifty pages in length depending on the child's age.

Give them five minutes to read as much of the book as possible.

Stop them at five minutes and ask them to tell you what they remember.

And be sure to give them the reward you promised them.

You can expand this exercise in the next session and challenge them to read TWO books of the same length.

As with any speed reading program or learning program, practice is very important.

Schedule sessions with your child often and be sure to practice each of the exercises I've given you so that they become more comfortable with the techni□ues.

* Exercise to increase and widen the 'seeing' lens.

* Exercise using imagination and visualization.

* Exercise to 'chunk' information by signaling in 'five second' increments

* Exercise to read a book in five minutes

Continue scheduled practice sessions for one to two months until the child has grasped and solidified the concepts in her mind.

After that, they can use the new techni□ues every day to improve their reading speed and comprehension.

Is the Computer a Viable Tool for Teaching Children to Read

For many years the alphabet has been taught using traditional methods which have worked very successfully and are responsible for the majority of us being literate. However, is it time to move on and take advantage of modern technology and the wide range of websites for kids which teach the alphabet, letter sounds and reading and spelling?

Games for kids have always been a great way of teaching the alphabet and they learn easily and without pressure or even knowledge of their increased awareness and many parents implement this in the home with the use of flash cards, books and kids games which stimulate the child's interest. These are known to be a success and are also popular with the children. But what about the computer? As adults, the majority of us have a computer at home which will be used for a variety of purposes and it is easy to see the appeal that it has for the children. The highly visual attraction is hard to resist and they often become keen to investigate. However, not many parents are keen to have their children spend hours playing computer games which give little or no educational instruction and often over stimulate their brains to no advantage. But how about using the computer to actually educate the children and teach them their alphabet and get them reading easily and without pressure?

Activities for kids cannot be replaced by a computer. Fact. Children need to be given activities away from the computer and this is also true when teaching the alphabet and learning to read. To leave the job entirely to a computer package would be to take away some of the practical elements of learning. Puzzles for kids are an important part of their lives and can never be replaced by a keyboard and screen. The tangible experience of doing a puzzle is irreplaceable. They stimulate minds at the same time as increasing dexterity - something which goes beyond using a keyboard and mouse. But I do believe that a combination of manual, traditional methods and computer software packages is a great system.

Children are attracted to computers on account of the colourful moving graphics. This is fun and fun is what appeals to kids. Many children would choose the computer over flashcards and books on account of this and this is the ammunition that software producers are using to gain popularity. Many of the programs, however have drawbacks and are not using well-grounded teaching techniues to educate the children. As children are such sponges when it comes to taking in information, it is easy to give them the wrong signals and information and this will become implanted into their minds and difficult to remove.

Some computer programmes for example have poor sound reproduction which can confuse the children. Letter sounds can be misleading and this can be a stumbling point right at the onset of learning the alphabet. Confusion is disastrous for a child's mind and it is easy to cause confusion but very difficult to clear up. The brain of a child is very accepting. They believe many things without uestion and if the phonetic alphabet is being badly pronounced and reproduced with poor sound uality this will become easily imprinted into their minds and accepted. It will then become difficult to change - you cannot just hit a delete button in their memories.

Yes, computers are a superb way to teach the alphabet, but make sure that the package that you choose is a good uality one. Check the pronunciation of the words and the sound quality. Make sure that the package is working at a gentle pace and covers all the aspects necessary for them and does not give half the information before moving on to the next step. Websites for kids will never be able to fully replace what they need in the way of stimulation and education. Children need to progress with tangible products such as books and flash cards to encourage dexterity and practical learning. A computer should not be seen as an alternative but as an aid. Neither should it be seen as a solitary tool for teaching. Sit with your child and make a time to spend together and encourage them to think as well as just look at the pretty graphics!

Make use of the facilities that technology is giving us but do not forget the pleasures of books and puzzles for kids.

CHAPTER 7- LEARNERS AND THE PHONICS SYSTEM

With Synthetic Phonics systems in place in most classrooms in the English-speaking world, many more children are picking up literacy with relative ease. However, 20% of children reach 11 and are not able to pass a reading test. Many children are still not grasping phonics.

Why is this the case?

Children, like the rest of us, have differing learning styles. We all automatically use the parts of the brain that work best for us. The more we use those particular parts, the more they develop and become more highly-functioning, often to the detriment of other areas. When this scientific truth is applied to literacy, it can have a surprising and unwanted result.

The act of reading is a highly complex task involving different cortexes of the brain - the visual, the auditory and a few in between! Visual learners seem to be at particular risk when it comes to learning how to read successfully, though at first, this risk may be well hidden. Children with this visual learning style will usually succeed in early literacy tasks, like learning the alphabet and simple words through sight-memorisation and repetition. Both of these methods appeal to their brain's highly engaged visual capacity.

But they are using a technique that will eventually fail them as their reading material grows in length an vocabulary.

As the text gets more complex they can no longer reliably use their sight memory or the context as a trigger and so they begin to guess very wildly. Meanwhile, many of their classmates are progressing while they struggle and their confidence eventually collapses.

Most reading recovery schemes are an intensive application of the same learning approach that has already failed, using a 'do more of the same' philosophy.

In contrast, a Guided Phonetic Reading technique seems to play to the strengths of these children, using their bright visual processing cortex as a tool to teach.

By presenting them with visually memorable characters which reflect phonemes (sounds) which can then serve as tools to decode words - instead of memorising the shape of the words themselves - we are turning abstract information (such as the phonemes) into something the children can grasp and hang on to in their visual cortex.

Through Guided Phonetic Reading, children are weaned off their habit of jumping to a guess rather than scanning each word to match the letter patterns with the sound patterns.

Before learning to read- phonics

Even before your children get to school you can give them a great start in learning to read by helping them develop their skills in phonics - or the ability to discriminate and use speech sounds. English speech is made up of 44 sounds combined in different ways, and a child's ability to be able to hear and use these sounds is of vital importance in their ability to speak, listen and write. Below are a number of way in which you can help your child develop these skills before they even reach school age.

1)Listen to sounds in your environment. If you are taking a walk with your child or playing in the park, listen to the sounds around you and discuss them. Can you hear the magpie? How is the sound it makes different from the sound another bird makes?

2)Play a 'what sound is that' game. Hide several objects with well known sounds e.g. keys, s☐ueaky toy, an instrument. Make the objects noise and ask the children what it is. Alternatively, demonstrate each sound before you hide them, and tell the children the objects get revealed if they can remember the sound they make. Keep the children guessing till they have revealed all the objects.

3)Have your child use musical instruments. These do not have to be professionally purchased instruments, they can make their own. Having musical instruments teaches children to hear different notes and the timing of sounds. Play two notes and ask the child if they are the same or different, which one is higher? Which one is louder?

4)Participate in action songs with your children e.g. 'going on a bear hunt', or 'twinkle twinkle little star'. The combination of actions and music provides a fun, multisensory approach and re☐uires careful listening to the music.

5)Rhyme all the time. Read books with rhyming verse, play rhyming games (how many words can you think of that rhyme with a cat?) and ask your child if words rhyme or not. Rhyming is a great way for children to think about the individual sounds that make up a word.

6)Use alliteration and concentrate on the initial sound of a word. For example, you could play 'I spy' but use sounds instead of letters 'I spy something beginning with Ssssss...'

7)Get children familiar with the sounds they can make with their voices. See if they can imitate silly sounds you make with your voice.

8)Play with breaking up the sounds in words and combining them again. Ask your child, what word these sounds make - 'c-a-t', or ask them to 'go and get your c-oa-t'. Have a competition to see who can come up with the word with the most sounds in it.

9)And most of all, read to your child. Reading has positive impacts far beyond your child just learning to read, and if you get the right books it should be fun for you as well. You can use many of the other techni□ues while reading.

These techni□ues seem simple but thinking about and playing with speech sounds is a critical first stage of reading. If children do not understand that speech is made up of separate sounds, they have great trouble understanding that different sounds map onto different letter combination's, and that is how we spell and read. When children are young their brains are deciding which sounds are important and which are not, and it loses the ability to hear unfamiliar sound combination's as we get older. That is why it is much harder to learn a language when you are older. So it is crucial we teach our children good phonetic skills while they are still very young.

Choosing a Good Phonics Reading Program

Teaching a child to read is a beautiful thing. When we teach our children to read we open up a whole new world to them. Now all the lines and symbols that have been surrounding them make sense. It is such a wonderful and fascinating journey to give a child the gift of literacy, but how do parents get started?

Many parents want to give their child a head start in learning to read. They do not want to wait and hope their child gets it in school. But how does a parent that is not a teacher even begin teaching their child to read? That is where a good program is necessary. A well planned phonics program does not rely on the parent to be the teacher, but rather the guide. The parent only need follow the instructions that are laid out and explain them to the child. Any parent that knows how to read can teach their own child to read with a good phonics program.

So what makes one program better than another? Well, the goal of teaching your chiild is to learn to read and comprehend it □uickly. This means that the program you select should have your child reading words within days of beginning the program. Any program that requires months of preparation before actual reading begins should be avoided. A child is excited by their success. If your child is learning to read words within the first few lessons, they will be motivated to continue on in their studies. Also children learn best through play, so make sure the program includes lots of games and songs.

The most ingenious way of teaching children to read that I have ever see in through pictures. When a new sound is introduced, it is first done with a picture. This makes it simple for the child to recall the sound that they are learning, since the picture helps them to identify it immediately.

For example, the sound for the letter a is the beginning sound for the word apple. The child is taught to say the short a sound whenever they see the picture with the apple. The letter is shown on the back and the child progresses from reading the pictures to reading the actual letters, but the visual clues make it easy enough to teach children as young as 3 years old.

When deciding to teach your child to read, do some research online and find out what is working for others.

CHAPTER 8- POSITIVE MINDSET- AN IMPORTANT TOOL FOR BOTH THE PARENT AND THE CHILD

Regardless of the topic, experts in almost every field are linking our degree of success with our mindset.

Highly successful marketing gurus and business coaches like Sandi Krakowski and Dr. Joe Vitale top their lists of "Keys to Success" with maintaining a positive mindset about what we believe, what we tell ourselves and what we think about our level of success.

Tony Robbins, renowned motivational speaker, has made a huge impact on millions of people's lives by inspiring them to change their thoughts. The most influential and powerful woman in the world, Oprah Winfrey, attributes her immeasurable success to the fact that she always believed she would do great things...in other words, she had a mindset that said she could and would do whatever she wanted.

And the proof of the importance of acquiring and maintaining a positive attitude and mindset is everywhere. Even hardcore scientists who are fact-based thinkers have jumped on the bandwagon given the evidence through the studies of Quantum Physics.

Understanding and acknowledging the tremendous impact our mindset has in every phase of our lives has motivated parents to look for tools to instill the skills to create a positive mindset in their children.

I was raised to live life according to the theory that we are all responsible for what happens in our lives based on what we think and believe. I was taught that if we think and focus on negativity, negativity is what we will get. On the other hand, if we look for what is positive and joyful, we can expect more joy and happiness. I will also stand firm on the fact that when we do maintain a positive mindset, life is happier, more fulfilling and much more in line with what we desire it to be than if we choose to see things in from a negative perspective.

I hear from a great deal of parents wanting help on how to guide their children to have a positive mindset...many are working on gaining this for themselves but are at a loss as to how to convey it to their children.

One of the ways I share with parents is to teach children that thoughts are not absolute. Thoughts are negotiable. They can be observers of their thoughts and only accept the positive and discard the negative.

In addition to recognizing the negative physical effects of negative thoughts, children must also learn that what they think does not define who they are..... they do not have to claim every thought as being part of them.

"You have the capacity to choose what you think about. If you choose to think about past hurts, you will continue to feel bad. While it's true you can't change the effect past influences had on you once, you can change the effect they have on you now." ~Gary McKay, Ph.D.

Teaching Kids to Think Positively

The power of positive thinking is touted in the popular press and the therapist's office. Most adults understand that the way we think about a situation can change the way we experience it. But what about children? When and how do they learn about the connection between thoughts, feelings, and experiences?

Research has shown that this awareness evolves in early childhood and matures over many years. When children are three to four years old, they can identify emotions that occur in many typical situations. They know that birthday parties are happy times and scoldings are not. By the time they are five to six years old they have an increased awareness of the connection between thinking and feeling. By age seven many children understand that people can interpret the same situation in different ways.

Training children to recognize the benefits of positive thinking and disadvantages of negative thinking may not only help children feel better emotionally during stressful life circumstances, but may also provide physical and mental health benefits by decreasing the physical toll of stress.

A recent study investigated whether the developmental changes that take place between ages 5 to 10 would affect children's knowledge of the effects of thinking positively and whether this would, in turn, affect a child's emotional response to a situation.

Ninety children were divided into three age groups: 5-6, 7-8, and 9-10 year-olds. They were introduced to three pairs of characters who experienced a typically positive situation (getting a new pet), a negative situation (breaking an arm), and a neutral situation (meeting a new teacher).

One character within each pair had a positive thought that framed the event in a positive light, and one had a negative thought that framed the event in a negative light. For example, one character with a broken arm thought about having his friends sign his cast, while the other thought about how uncomfortable the cast was going to be.

The children were asked to report on each character's feelings: How does the character feel right now? Why does the character feel that way? They were also asked to explain why one character felt better than or the same as another character. The children's explanations were categorized as situation explanations, meaning that the situation caused the emotion; or mental state explanations, meaning that the characters' thoughts, desires, or preferences were the reasons that the character felt an emotion.

Children in every age group predicted characters' thinking positive as opposed to negative thoughts would have different emotions even though both characters experienced the same objective event, according to the study. The eight- to ten- year olds were more aware that reframing events either positively or negatively could affect a person's emotional experience, but all the children, regardless of age, seemed to believe that when events were negative, thinking positively was not enough to make a person feel good.

"The strongest predictor of children's knowledge about the benefits of positive thinking — besides age — was not the child's own level of hope and optimism, but their parents'," said Christi Bamford, assistant professor of psychology at Jacksonville University, who led the study when she was at the University of California, Davis.

The findings point to parents' role in helping children learn how to use positive thinking to feel better when things get tough. Bamford notes, "...[P]arents should consider modeling how to look on the bright side."

The researchers concluded that children as young as five years old had begun to develop the skills to understand how positive and negative reframing could change a person's response to a situation. They suggest that training children to recognize the benefits of positive thinking and disadvantages of negative thinking may not only help children feel better emotionally during stressful life circumstances, but may also provide physical health benefits by decreasing the physical toll of stress. Parents, teachers, coaches, and others who teach and care for children can model positive reframing for children to help them learn this valuable life skill.

Building a Loving, Learning, & Language Rich Environment Through Play and Positive Daily Interaction

Building a language rich environment is, on the face of it, an easy thing to do. Unfortunately, in today's busy households and with the busy lifestyles of parents who have to work full-time, it is harder to find the time to spend with your children than many of us realize. However, there are many activities that you can use on a daily basis to teach language in everyday situations, enhance your child's speech and language development and create a good environment for learning.

Make time for your children!

Children learn speech and language through listening, watching, exploring, copying, initiating, responding, playing and interacting with others. For those first few years most of the important interaction is going to be between the child and their parents, carers and maybe siblings. Finding time to spend with your children and have a shared focus is very important if you want to help them to develop their speech, language and social skills. One-to-one time will benefit your child in the long term.

You are doing your child a disservice if you have spare time, but put them in front of the TV. There are a few (and only a few!) children's TV programs that are in any way educational. Your child is more likely to learn about things from one-to-one playtime with his parent or carer. TV and video games are passive entertainment and do not encourage any interaction. Studies now show that children who watch too much TV in their early years are more likely to have difficulties with attention and listening when they reach school age. However, there are few educative programs your child can watch on TV.

There is also evidence to show that if the child uses a dummy/pacifier, their speech can be delayed. Speech can be delayed because the child is not speaking, and because the development of the child's oral musculature may be affected by the constant sucking of a dummy.

Building an environment that helps your child's language develop:

Building a language rich environment is about using every opportunity to use language, to interact, to share a focus, to talk, to take turns. Building a language rich environment is also about building a nurturing environment, giving your child love and affection and building their self-confidence. And finally, it is about building a learning environment, creating a place where love, language and learning can all take place together.

So what do you do to create this environment? Well firstly look at yourself and how you are communicating:

Think about your child's language level:

One of the biggest things to be aware of when using language around your young child is the level and complexity of the language you use. Think about their age and how much language they use. A young child will generally understand more words than he uses in speech. You can use milestones charts to get a broad idea of your child's language level. Assuming your child is developing along normal lines think about where to pitch your language. For instance, if your child is aged 2 years and 6 months and is able to follow a short instruction containing 2 key words, be mindful of this when you talk to her. If you use long sentences she will not understand you. If your child does have difficulty understanding, just use key words, more intonation, and gesture, or point as you say the words.

When talking to your child, try to talk about things that are in context or that the child can see, so they can use these things as a reference. Talk slowly and put emphasis on the key words if they are in a sentence, and use lots of intonation to help emphasize meaning. Give the child more time to respond than you would with older children or an adult. Younger children may need a little longer to process your speech and formulate an answer of their own. This is even more important if your child has difficulties acquiring language. If your child has language difficulties, or receptive language delay, limiting your words, giving them lots of time to process language, and using lots of gesture is essential.

Take a step back and feed in language during play:

You can enhance your child's development of language by sometimes taking a step back during play and letting them take the lead. This gives the child control of their environment and builds their confidence. Although you are still involved in the play you are not dictating what is happening. However, you can still be feeding language into the play as it is happening. So the take-away here is not to feel you have to fill in any gaps of silence, just watch and listen and add language.

For instance, if your daughter is playing with her dolls, just watch, add language to her words and dictate some of her actions.

Chloe: dolly tea

Mum: the dolly's drinking tea, and that one is having a sandwich

Chloe: sandwich

Mum: mmm sandwich, whats it got in it...jam, a jam sandwich mmm

Chloe: mmmm sandwich

Mum: mmmmm jam sandwich yummy

Chloe: more tea

Mum: more tea for dolly and teddy is drinking tea too

Chloe: cake

Mum: oooh, are they getting cake too, yummy

Chloe: yummy cake

Mum: yum yum yum eating lots of cake (rubs tummy)

This is a simple example and although mum is only adding a few new words she is acknowledging her daughters words and she is expanding on her sentences. Chloe can hear her words being put into longer more grammatical sentences and a couple of verbs are added (eating and drinking). Chloe remains in charge throughout the game, she leads the game and the dictates what is happening. This situation allows her control so there is no pressure on her to communicate and the communication environment is a relaxed and nurturing place.

Think about the language you use during play:

Children do not learn language by having an adult continually asking them to name various items. Children learn by hearing words and linking them to things. So it is a good idea to feed language into play, rather than asking your child to name every toy they are playing with. Adding language is an easy thing to do and can be done in all types of different situations, not just play. You can comment on what the child sees, commentate on what your child is doing, or expand on what they have said e.g.

Child· car

Adult: that's right, it's a car, a fast car

or

Adult: that's right, it's a car, a red car,and there is a blue car

Child: cat

Adult: yes, the cat is climbing (gesture the actions, and emphasize the key words cat and climbing)

The other way to add language is to describe what your child is doing during play. For instance, if your daughter is playing with her dolls in the dolls house, give a little commentary:

Jane: dolly

Dad: dolly's going in the house

Jane: sit

Dad: dolly's sitting down

Jane: drink

Dad: dolly's got a cup, she is drinking tea drink tea

Jane: tea

Dad: yes, dolly is drinking tea... and now she is eating cake

The temptation here is to ask a ⬜uestion, such as "what is dolly doing" or "what is dolly drinking". This immediately puts the emphasis on the child, and they then have to stop their play and respond. By just commenting, you are not putting any pressure on your child to communicate so the play is more relaxed. The child is also able to play on their own terms and control the game.

Having a shared focus:

The above examples show the importance of having a shared focus. This is important because not only are you giving the child a point of reference when you talk about things, but the child is learning listening and using attention skills. These skills are vitally important for the child when they attend school and the early years are key years for developing these skills. The best ways to develop these skills is to spend time with your child, talk and play with the child, and have a shared focus.

Try and develop a shared focus with your child whenever you are engaging in communication.

Share the moment and look at things together. Make sure you are at the child's level and have good eye contact. It is important to notice what interests your child and what they are focusing on, and then comment on it. This helps create a shared focus, shows the child that you are interested and allows them to link language to the things they are looking at when you comment.

Also, make sure you attend to the child's vocalizations or attempts at speech and try and translate them. If you are able to acknowledge and understand your child's attempts at speech it encourages them to attempt more, and at the same time, you are providing a good model of the speech. If you can't understand your child, repeat back her word, but at the same time point to things you think she may be trying to say.

Most daily activities can involve a shared focus:

Shopping: tell your child what item you are looking for, that way you can turn your attention to the items on the shelves and name some of them. You can name them for your child if she does not recognize them.

Reading books: this is an excellent way to have a shared focus. Look at the book, talk about the pictures and read the story.

Cooking: make a cake together, talk about the ingredients and what you are doing (stirring, mixing, pouring etc). Follow a recipe step by step (sequencing skills).

Toys: have a tea party with your daughter and her dolls. Describe what everyone is doing (but don't ask questions and let your daughter take the lead). Do the voices for some of the dolls and add language that way.

Pretend play to develop language and social skills:

Pretend play is another great way to develop your child's imagination and add lots of language at the same time. Letting your child lead the game also gives them a sense of control and can build self confidence. Here is an example of how a dad and his son pretend to be firemen and all the different ways that this can be educational for the child (see below). I will also give you some other examples.

Example 1. - Firemen

You are a dad and you have 15 minutes to spend with your 4-year old son. You decide to be firemen and imagine that you have got a call to put out a fire in a big building. Firstly let's think about the Language we will be using:

Nouns: fire, fireman, hat, boots, hose, water, fire engine, smoke, ladder

Verbs: drive, climb, run, jump, smell

Adjectives: hot, wet

Prepositions: in front, in, on

Social skills: Turn-taking and shared focus

Self confidence: Let your son be the chief fireman, let him give you the orders

Affection: Give him a hug to celebrate when you put the fire out and save all the people

How easy was that!! This is just one short simple little role play where a boy is playing, learning, listening and using language, building social skills, building self confidence, and bonding with his dad. Dad only needed 15 minutes out of his day to do it. It is not hard, you can do it in short bursts when you have little pieces of time.

Example 2. Dress up for the ball

Have a dress-up with your daughter and imagine you are going to a ball. Language used:

Nouns: dress, shoes, ball, make-up, hair etc

Verbs: dress, dance, fasten etc

Adjectives: pretty, elegant etc

Prepositions: on, in, under etc

Social skills: A shared focus, talking about the ball

These are simple examples and with a bit of imagination could be expanded in all sorts of ways, but it illustrates that it is easy to create playtime situations, that are fun and also can be used to positively promote speech and language skills, social skills and build confidence.

Body language and using gesture:

Try to use body language and gesture when you speak. This helps the child understand what you are saying, but it may also teach them to do the same so that they can make themselves understood more effectively. Body language plays a huge part in helping others gain meaning from what we say, this is a good skill for children to learn, especially if their speech is not clear in the early year.

Answering your children's questions and turn-taking:

Children are inquisitive and it is important to always take the time to answer their questions. Answering questions creates a 2-way communication process, because you both have a turn and you both have to wait and use good listening skills. Sometimes children go through a phase of asking "why" in response to everything you say. If this becomes a habit (rather than a genuine question), respond with your answer and then ask them a question. This creates a turn-taking opportunity and at the same time making the child to respond to a question. If you want your children to learn language and develop speech and social skills - TURN OFF THE TV AND TALK TO THEM AND PLAY WITH THEM!!!

CONCLUSION

Throughout the different phases of my life, I have constantly being amazed at the positive influence of reading and writing with our children. As a former educator, the advantages of exposure to reading at home became obvious to me. Everyone can easily appreciate the strong learning foundation created by reading to preschoolers.

Word recognition, comprehension abilities, and listening skills are all fostered through the parent-child reading experience. Educators who have studied the topic agree that a link is evident between academic success and exposure to reading at a young age. I have witnessed evidence to support this in my days in the classroom.

I observed the greatest benefits of preschool reading, however, through my experiences as a parent. The greatest benefits of preschool reading is in the experience itself. It comes from the cuddle, the closeness and the joy of the moment.

If you are a parent, you understand that sentiment. If you are not a parent, reflect for a moment on your own childhood memories of reading with your parents. I do not have to say another word to convince you of the importance of reading to preschoolers.

During the preschool years, children may ask to read the same book again and again. My three year old son used to ask for the same book at least three times a day for a period of time. I'm certain there are parents out there who can relate to that experience.

Maybe even a parent or two could relate to my thinking that this story might be becoming a little boring! My son liked it for a particularly funny phrase which it contained -"And there in the woods a piggy wig stood with a ring in the end of his nose - with a ring in the end of his nose!" It made him laugh so heartily that all of my boredom slipped easily away!

My daughter was so proud when she could reverse the reading situation and read a book to me! At 3, she really didn't recognize each word. She memorized it from so frequently reading the story. She knew exactly when to turn the pages.

At this point, reading had not provided her with word recognition skills. I feel, however, that it had already provided her with confidence and self-esteem. She was so proud of her accomplishments!

She continued to excel in public speaking throughout her school years and developed into a very confident young lady. I know many factors are at play in a child's development. I give a lot of credit, however, to those reading experiences and the subse□uent self-esteem which it fostered in her.

Sometimes our reading experiences with our children do not even have to involve books. You can "read" a child a story from the script in your mind. Think about it for a moment! Is there not a touch of a writer in us all? Do we not all have vivid imaginations? How many of us keep journals? How many participate in online forums?

My son preferred the stories from the imagination without the printed text. He preferred for me to invent my own stories. No, that did not provide him with word recognition skills. Yet it still provided the valuable reading "experience."

As well, it dismisses the abstract idea of author and puts it in a more tangible realm. If Mommy can write in her mind, then so can I! My youngest son developed a passion for writing and wrote an entire play while in high school. Reading and writing are intertwined as one entity. One skill fosters the other! The love of one supports the love of the other!

Most children enjoy books when they are given the opportunity to explore. Previously, I was a Discovery Toys representative. I organized play groups for children. Children would gravitate towards the books. At times, a flashy cover or interesting feature would attract them to a book. Yet it was the joy of reading which would ultimately keep their interest.

Even as a grandparent, I continued to create stories for my grandchild. I could not read with him very often in person as he lived in another province. I decided to send him stories via email - complete with graphics and animation. The feedback I received was that they provided lots of enjoyment. The enjoyment was mutual! This was the inspiration for an exciting business venture.

Instead of providing stories just to my family, I could broaden my enjoyment and create stories for others. There is no shortage of access to children's stories so I decided on a new twist to children's e-stories - uni☐ue children's personalized e-stories! Personalized stories are thought to be a self-esteem enhancer.

Some personalized stories in the marketplace just contain the child's name.(or their friends' names). Yet the children still learn to recognize their names. They gain self-esteem from reading a story about themselves. Personalized stories can be the impetus to encourage a child to keep a journal or write a story about themselves or their family or friends.

With my personalized e-stories, I decided to try to tweak the children's interest in reading. I provide an uni☐ue story (some themes) for each child. Each story contains 8 - 12 elements of the child's life ranging from the simple - favorite color - to the more complex - special wish or dream. Each story is as individual as each child.

Any extra incentive which can encourage children to enjoy reading has to have a positive outcome. Instilling a love of reading in a child is giving them a gift which will last a lifetime. We pass down our recipes from generation to generation. Let's not forget to do likewise with our books and their joys!

Stories, read or written, don't have to cost a cent. They can be accessed from library sources. Yet they are they are always free anyway in our imagination! So regardless whether or not you purchase stories or books, remember the reading experience and Please Read With Your Child!

Inculcating the reading habit in children

Books are the ☐uietest and most constant of friends; they are the most accessible and wisest of counselors, and the most patient of teachers. ~Charles W. Eliot

Charles Eliot had his facts right. Anyone who has befriended the written word would never be lonely. All booklovers know that they can live several lives, travel innumerable places and do myriad things through their books. You get to see the perspective of another person and find out that you are not the absolute authority on the topic.

Today our living rooms have been invaded by the television and computer. Children spend all the free time glued to either of them.

Books teaches a lot to the kids. They expand their vocabularies, helping them later in life. The command of the language increases many fold. It gives a boost to the child's imagination, letting the mind reach the unthinkable and increasing the creativity. Reading about many things vastly improves the child knowledge store. Say, for instance, you learn more about Africa but reading an interesting story than by the dry course books.

Parents despair, trying to introduce them to the wonderful world of books. However, everything is not lost with a thimbleful of common sense, a little patience and bushelful of love parents can introduce good reading habits to their kids.

Fix a time for reading

Keep about half an hour daily reserved as reading time. This can be just before bed time or any other time suitable to both. Initially, let them read the books you had recounted as children. The story line will be familiar and it will be easy for them to pick out the words.

Start young

Interest in books cannot be generated overnight. It is a slow process where in the child learns to fall in love with the enchanted world of the written world. If the habit of reading is inculcated at the earliest, this will develop slowly as the child grows. Parents have to start as soon as the child is able to understand. Read out stories to your two year old child. Slowly phase out this story telling to story reading.

Baby steps

Parentts should be realistic in their expectations. Do not think that the child will jump into reading the very first time they get their hands on the book. The first few times they may falter with pronunciations. Gently correct them. They may even read through the whole page without understanding a word. Instant of explaining the whole book to them, make their brains work. Ask easy questions about the story. Eventually they will get the hang of deciphering books.

Read

It is very important to teach the kids by setting an example. Ensure that the children see you read. If you read books your children will automatically do the same. It is very difficult to convince a child to read copiously if the parents never pick up a book. Not only it will be an inspiration but also the kids will find reading together a lot of fun.

Get books on subjects of interest

If the child is a great Pooh fan, get some books on that character. The markets abound with a variety of things related to cartoons. Do a little market survey and get the books of the particular character. Ensure that the books are colorful and picturesque. The print should be large as reading small print can be tedious. Go through the books before buying. The words should be of a level understandable by your child. Too easy or too tough books distract the children very easily.

Install aids

There are many supporting aids the parents can utilize to encourage reading. Set up a bulletin board and put cartoons with funny comments on it. Pin a small limerick or poetry on it for your child to read. You can get an audio book set too. This has a story recorded on tape along with the printed book. The children can catch the nuances of pronunciation as they read along. Put notes in the Tiffin box. Get vocabulary- building games on the computer.

Universal Reading Time

Do not restrict reading to the confines of your room. Utilize the abundance of words floating all around us. Point out the words on the hoardings on the way. Ask the child to read out the credits on the cinema poster. Telling the headlines from the newspaper is a very good way to learn. While you are waiting for the doctor to arrive, they can read up the pamphlets. At the restaurant, let them read the menu and decide on the order. Ask them to decipher the instructions on the new game.

Do not push

Try all this in a very casual manner. If the child gets feeling that she is being pushed towards reading, she will stall like an adamant horse. It should all seem like a wildly interesting game. Remember Tom Sawyer! Say for instance, while waiting for the doctor, don't push the pamphlet in the kids hand and order her too read. Instead, say very, very casually (a bored voice is a must), "There are four words starting with ch in this pamphlet." Immediately the child will try to find out the fact for herself and find a few more words to boot.

These techniques are just general aids to help the children read more. As a parent you have to show enthusiasm towards their new activity. Correct them gently, when wrong. Show enthusiasm and appreciation when the child wants to read. It is a good idea to buy books as gifts and incentive. Discuss the book the child has just read. Talk about her favorite character in the book. If there is a movie made on the particular book, make it a point to take her to it.

Don't force, guide. As soon as the child learns that she has to read, it becomes another subject to study, a tiresome chore. Reading should be introduced as a delightful pastime and not rigorous punishment.

So, go ahead, introduce your kids to the written word and they will never be lonely again.

The End

Made in the USA
Middletown, DE
25 February 2019